Reading Togeth

D1351977

Guess
What
I am

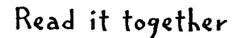

Read it together

This enjoyable peep-hole book invites children to play with it like a game. To guess each animal they need to search the pages, discovering more information along the way.

I want to turn the page.

First tell me what animal you think it will be.

It can't be a leopard because it hasn't got spots.

Could it be a zebra with those stripes?

Take time to talk about the picture clues for each animal. Talk through what animals it could and couldn't be.

You're right, it *is* a tiger! How did you know?

I think it's a tiger.

Both the words and the pictures give clues to help children guess what the animal is likely to be. Encourage your child to talk about the clues that help them guess.

Throughout this information book there is a pattern of questions, descriptions and answers to make it easier for children to join in with the reading. Encourage your child to say the repeated parts with you.

Children enjoy talking about books during the reading and afterwards. They often have questions to ask or comments to make. This book might remind them of animals they've seen and could prompt a farm or zoo visit!

First published 1998 by Walker Books Ltd
87 Vauxhall Walk, London SE11 5HJ

This edition published 2007

2 4 6 8 10 9 7 5 3 1

Text ● 1998 Walker Books Ltd
Illustrations ● 1998 Anni Axworthy
Introductory and concluding notes ● 2001 CLPE/LB Southwark

This book has been typeset in Joe Overweight

Printed in China

All rights reserved

British Library Cataloguing in Publication Data:
a catalogue record for this book is available
from the British Library

ISBN 978-1-4063-1410-6

www.walkerbooks.co.uk

Guess
What
I am

Illustrated by
Anni Axworthy

WALKER BOOKS
AND SUBSIDIARIES

LONDON · BOSTON · SYDNEY · AUCKLAND

What am I?

I'm a kind of cat,
like this kitten.

This is
my stripy
fur.

in the jungle.

Tigers are the biggest cats in the world.

What am I?

I'm a kind of fish,
but I don't live in a bowl.

e lots

ery

teeth.

cars.

A Great white
shark has two rows of teeth
at the top and two at the bottom.

What am I?

I like to gnaw on things,
just like these mice do.

is my wide
lat tail.

rivers.

I'm
bea

Beavers make their dams out of logs and twigs.

What am I?

I have wings like this parrot, but I can't fly.

This is my
favourite food.

This is
my beak.

I live near the icy South Pole.

There are 18 different sorts
of penguin. I'm a King penguin.

What am I?

This puppy is a kind of dog,
and so am I.

Foxes make their dens
in towns as well as in
the countryside.

Animal Trail

Can you find the animal who builds dams across rivers?

Can you find the animal who is a kind of cat?

Can you find
the animal who
is as long as
two cars?

Can you find
the animal whose
favourite food
is fish?

Can you find
the animal who
lives in a den
underground?

All our names have got muddled up. Can you help us to sort them out?

Beaver

Penguin

Fox

Tiger

Shark

Read it again

Act it out
Gather a collection of toy animals to match those in the book. Children can use them to retell the book or create their own story.

I am the biggest animal of all and I can ROAR at you!

This word says penguin.

There it is!

Matching game
Look at the back of the book together and play the matching game.

And look! So has the beaver.

The mouse has got whiskers.

Spot the animal
Look through the book together, taking it in turns to notice details about the animals. Which animals have beaks, tails or fur? Which animals can swim?

Make a peep-hole
You can make your own peep-hole by cutting a hole in a piece of paper or card. Place it over pictures of animals in magazines or books and ask children to guess what is in the pictures.

What am I?
You can play "What am I?" games on car journeys or at home. Adults can begin by describing an animal for others to guess. Clues can get harder as your child becomes used to the game! Take it in turns to start.

Make a poster
Your child can make a poster of their favourite animal. You could help them by writing down what they say about it.